SLG POCKET BOOKS 1

THE RECONCILERS

Sister Isabel SLG

SLG Press

SLG Pocket Books 1

ISBN 978-0-7283-0354-6
SLG pocket books ISSN 2978-8633 (Print)
SLG pocket books ISSN 2978-8641 (eBooks)

Edited and typeset in Bembo Std by Julia Craig-McFeely

Biblical quotations are taken from the New Revised Standard Version of the Bible unless otherwise noted.

Cover image: Baptistry Window, Coventry Cathedral
Page 1: Basalt relief of Simeon the Elder, Berlin, Staatliche Museen zu Berlin.

SLG Press
Convent of the Incarnation
Fairacres • Oxford
www.slgpress.co.uk

Printed by
Grosvenor Group Ltd, Loughton, Essex
SLG Press Publications are printed on FSC Certified sustainable papers.

CONTENTS

Acknowledgements

This text was first published in two parts in *Crucible, The Journal of the Church Assembly Board for Social Responsibility* (July 1969), 107–112 and (May 1970), 66–71. This revised and updated version was first published in *Fairacres Chronicle*, 58/2 (Winter 2025), 35–48.

THE
RECONCILERS

THE RECONCILERS
SISTER ISABEL SLG

A Sign of Being

Early in the fourth century, in the Syrian and African deserts where the Hellenic cities of Alexander's dream had long ago become centres of Roman imperial power, there could be seen, here and there on the outskirts, certain men who sat or stood on the tops of pillars, engaged in perpetual adoration and intercession, in defending the faith and, we are told, in the reconciliation of enemies. At a time of fierce debate about God these men had something to say, and they said it, as became their solid incarnational faith, with the whole of themselves, by climbing on top of a pillar and staying there for good. Probably in that 'land of sand and ruin and gold'[1] their action was less startling

---

[1] From Algernon Charles Swinburne, 'The Triumph of Time' (1866).

than might be imagined. All the same they were not ignored; food was passed up to them, and in bitter weather, blankets, but no one suggested they should come down and, most significant of all, people came to them to be reconciled. For it was somehow understood that in spite of their singular withdrawal from it, they were neither hostile nor indifferent to society, but more deeply, more responsibly concerned with it than most other people. As a place to live, the pillar was certainly crude to the point of absurdity, but as a theological statement it could bear closer examination.

What the stylites were saying in their lonely, splendid standing was what Elijah had said hundreds of years before: 'God lives and I stand before his face' (1 Kgs 17:1)—that was the first and adequate motive for the gesture; they stood literally for God in an unbroken affirmation. But they stood also in God and with God. They took to the tops of their pillars wills so schooled in self-forgetfulness, minds and hearts so enlarged by pondering on God's creative and redemptive love, that all their energies were drawn to a single point of longing, a single intention that all men everywhere should respond and accept that love, so absolute, so total, that by comparison with its final shout from the Cross: 'It is finished', nothing else seemed ever really to have happened.

Cosmic Re-integration

In the incarnate Lord, eternity came into time; in his great Passover from death to life he reconstituted the whole human race in a quite new relationship as sons of the Father, brothers of the Saviour, sharers and companions of the life-giving Spirit. Because in Christ's obedience the power of a perfect love was present to reverse disobedience at the uttermost root of responsibility, in the free will of a man. Immeasurable results followed for all men from his death, his resurrection and his return to the Father. That native dimension of his being, which in his preaching he had called 'The Kingdom' was from now on wide open for anyone prepared to choose the narrow path of union with his sacrifice in baptism and eucharistic living. In his church he no longer has followers, but only members, limbs, parts of himself, for whom 'living is Christ' (Phil. 1:21), and whose task, in the power of his spirit, is to extend to every aspect of history and every fragment of experience, the news of his reconciling love, until in the end of time the last citizen of the kingdom has been gathered in.

It is against this background of cosmic reintegration that the action of the stylites can be seen not as an ascetic quirk from remote times, but rather as applied theology of a most radical kind. The point was not the precise mode of their identification with Christ, but its depth and reality, of which their solitude and exposure in the foolish-looking life of the pillar was a sign, just as the folly and weakness of the Cross spoke in palpable, historical terms of Christ's perfect union with his Father's will and of his infinite love for mankind. It was from this one-pointed gatheredness into God that they listened to what the Spirit was saying to the churches of their time and reached out in love to the passionate life of the city swarming below in its tenements and basilicas and theatres and banks—a microcosm of the whole created order held in the hand of God.

A Life of Answering

Today, as then and always, the central task of the Christian is still so to remain at that root where reversal has taken place, at the still centre, where God and man are reconciled, that all action and intercourse have their source and their completion in the stability of this anterior and paramount relationship which Christ called 'abiding' in him.

If Christians, in situations often so tragic and complex as to baffle analysis, are to bear witness to the Gospel of a redemption, love, everlasting life, they have somehow to set up in their own life the life of the pillar; to be in their own sphere of commitment and service—and in community and family life—gathering-points of attention and stillness before God. No one can fight their way to this stillness, but we can let ourselves be drawn there if we really want it, and implicit in this 'letting' is a liberating admission that we are not after all self-made, self-determined or self-sufficient, but the work of God's hands and the object of his mercy. It would be difficult, of course, to find an attitude more unpalatable to our contemporary 'pride of life' than that.

At least one theologian has become aware in the present of what he calls 'a widespread recovery of nerve' denoting the end of the God-ridden centuries that followed the celebrated 'loss of nerve' suffered by those in the third century in the discovery that there were limits to human knowledge.[2] Now, the unpredictable nuances of apparently boundless knowledge, actual and potential, cannot shake a growing confidence that eventually disease poverty, population, everything, can be got under control by means of resources increasingly submissive to science. In such a context 'creaturehood' means much the same as incapacity: it smacks of a

---

[2] Emmanuel Mesthene, 'Religious Values in the Age of Technology', *Concilium*, 6 (June 1967), 52–9.

whimpering sense of impotence that is unworthy of the stature and dignity of adult humanity.

But the person who has made the experiment of prayer by resolutely securing from the pressures of their crammed day one bit of time simply to spend with God for God's own sake, has already discovered the real human dignity which the foulest assaults of inhumanity cannot obliterate, nor any degree of 'cosmic mastery' add one cubit to. 'Dominion' was in any case something God gave to us, a responsible trust appropriate to the crowning, most characteristic work of creative love, 'his dearest, prized and priced'.[3] The essence of being a creature was not feebleness, and infantile security-drive, but a rational free-will response to an infinite, personal love, in which all the powers of body, intellect and spirit were to find their fulfilment. It is the joyful 'here we be' of the summoned stars, the boy Samuel listening in the dark; most of all it is the total surrender in the simplicity of faith of a young woman which admitted Divine Love into the created order in the form of a man, and made her the mother of God.

It was this divine entry into a humanity almost irretrievably twisted away from the life of response that

---

[3] Gerard Manley Hopkins, 'The Wreck of the Deutschland' (1875–6).

gave back, not as it originally was, but transfigured out of recognition, the lost power of loving God and loving all creation in God. The way of response was, from that moment, the way of God in us, a way of filial obedience which led, against the grain of every fallen impulse, through death to everlasting life. This way is set out step-by-step in the Gospel to be appropriated and lived, but it is in the central eucharistic act of the new humanity in Christ that each temporal word and action of the refracted glory that was his life on Earth races back into a single total presentness, the kingdom of an eternal now. Here the pilgrim people of God lift up their hearts in the joyful affirmation of what Christ has done and everlastingly is, by the presence of his Spirit in the church. The whole content of human life is offered and healed and made holy in Christ's perfect offering. He feeds his people with the bread of life and sends them out in the seal of the great 'Amen' to be him, to bring the life and values of his kingdom into their own kitchens and offices and committee rooms.

The Prayer of Gathering

The prayer of intercession is an organic function of this apostolic mediatorial life. It is not a more-or-less spasmodic exercise in remembering other people's needs before God, though it may necessarily take that form, but rather the inevitable overflow of love from a relationship, with God in Christ, in which all other relationships are seen and cherished in an ever-larger capacity for love. As in the Eucharist, the focus of attention is always God himself and not the pains and problems that are being brought to him for healing.

This attention is held in a frame of mind that is defined by faith, hope and love. That is to say, by Divine objective energies, properties of the Spirit who is the new life at the deepest level of personality; who inspires the prayer and pilots it through the channel of a surrendered will to the level of conscious petition. So to pray for peace—in one of the multiple war zones in the world today, in industry, in some estranged family or sick personality—may consist of nothing more than repeatedly and patiently recalling the attention to Christ who is our peace, who has made peace by the blood of his Cross, whose peace is not the absence of conflict, but a steadfast will to hold all aggression, all violence, in the obedience of his total union with the Father's will for peace.

Standing at the still centre where peace is made, responsive in faith to the love that draws on Calvary and to the tireless love that prays in the depth of his being, the intercessor will begin to know with an increasing sense of taking part, of being used, something of the cost of peace-making, something of the horror of separation in terms of Christ's willingness to answer it all with the lonely glory of his crucified love.

For us, who pray to bring this reconciliation into our service of a drifting world of strangers, it is always a case of *Credo 'ut intelligam'*. A readiness to act as if Christ really had conquered the world, as he said, has to precede very much understanding of what we are doing when we pray, or any conscious assurance that it will do the slightest good. Because life in Christ is always new, it is always experimental—'come and see'. It was with the irreducible simplicity of knowledge that the Starets Silouan the Athonite (1866–1938) could say: 'if a man will pray to God in humility that the Lord may enlighten him, the Lord will make known to him how greatly he loves mankind'.[4]

'How greatly he loves mankind'—that is the heart of the matter, and the only point of praying which would be otherwise only a meaningless suspension of the activity required of us. It is his love that heals, not our passionate indignation because life is callous and

---

[4] Silouan quoted in Archimandrite Sophrony, *The Undistorted Image: Staretz Silouan, 1866–1938* (Faith Press, 1958), 134.

cruel, and the world falling to bits. All passion outside the one saving passion tends to be divisive and partisan. The intercessor cannot afford the relief of taking sides. Our work is to stand at the heart of things, where the God-ward beam of the Cross meets the human-ward, world-ward beam in Christ's surrender, 'In stillness nailed to hold all time, all place, all circumstance in love's embrace.'[5] Even the passion of his caring is judged by its evanescence. As Auden noticed: 'like love we often weep, like love we seldom keep',[6] and if we are to sustain the adult work of intercession with at least as much dispassionate realism as any responsible person will bring to the discharge of their professional duties, it can only be in so far as such love as we can spare from our own concerns is invested and increased in the love that keeps, and goes on keeping, until the fullness of its eternal purpose is achieved.

We give ourselves not to our own ideals but to God's thirst for our hearts. Our intercession is not for this or that end, but for the infinite Kingdom, and to concentrate on limited specifics is a sterile badgering, empty of the relationship implied in asking 'in my name'. Real

---

[5] Gilbert Shaw, 'In Stillness Nailed …', in *The Face of Love* (Mowbrays, 1959).

[6] W. H. Auden, 'Law, Like Love' (1939).

prayer in the Name will be answered by some manifestation of the life and of the kingdom, which does not come by observation; some healing, some mercy, some transfiguring change in the situation which makes it manageable, bearable, and positively fruitful.

As mediators in Christ we have only one choice: to gather with him or to scatter apart from him, and intercession is simply the continual renewal of this choice. We can, in the very time and place of prayer, be drawn out into the multiple conflicts and needs pressing in on our perception, and quickly become swamps in the interplay of agony and argument that keeps them alive. On the other hand, we can encircle with the arms of our compassion everything that weighs on heart and brain and conscience, however trivial or tragic, and bring it, as women brought their children to Jesus, to the point where our faith is met by his faithfulness. When the intercessor is 'the gatherer gathered',[7] and our solidarity both with the deformed world and with the redeemed kingdom is held in the stillness where it is enough simply to affirm 'this is our God, we have waited for him' (Is. 25:9), then we and all we love and suffer for are at the heart of reality and the source of healing.

---

[7] Edwin Muir, 'The Question' (1941).

This point is the meeting place of the Christian community in time and in eternity; it is the focus of every eucharistic action and of every humble, minute extension of that action in daily life. It came into being here at the place of a skull—the place of dereliction out of which rose the irresistible vitality and power of the Son of God, the Lord of the churches.

His members live in the tension of what is passing away and what is being continually gathered into eternal life. If, in the sphere of the passing away, they look for comfort in numbers, even in the aggregate of Sunday communicants, they are more likely to find loneliness. Eleven men received the bread of life in the upper room, but only one stood with the women at the Cross to become the first Christian family: there is your son, there is your mother. It is the life instinct with affirmation of the kingdom as it penetrates and transfigures the ever-changing contents of human activity that bears its witness with arresting power. Seeking to explain the self-immolation of Buddhist monks as a sacrificial act of compassion for the sufferings of the Vietnamese people, the Venerable Nhất Hạnh says: 'the importance is not to take one's life, but to burn'.[8]

---

[8] Thích Nhất Hạnh, *Vietnam. The Lotus in the Sea of Fire* (SCM Press, 1967), 118. Self-immolation by Buddhist

We come back to the sign of a total love, and wherever this love is selflessly expressed it cannot be outside the saving act of redemption. Christians express this total love to which they have opened themselves in prayer by bringing their dependence on the Divine energy to bear directly on every aspect of their involvement in the shifting circumstances of the present—on each initiative and each response that life asks of them.

The inevitable conflict to which this will more and more expose them at every level and on all fronts will call for some attention in the second part of this essay. It is well to note at this point that it is always open to the Christian to follow a more accommodating way. The way of gathering with Christ will take us precisely as far as we are willing to be led. 'You are those,' said Jesus to his barely-comprehending disciples, 'who have stood by me in my trials' (Luke 22:28); but also, 'Are you able to drink the cup that I am about to drink?' (Matt. 20:22).

---

monks has occurred historically as a form of protest, most notably by Thích Quảng Đức in Vietnam in 1963, the seventh such suicide in south Vietnam that year, to protest against religious persecution, and more recently in the 2010s by numerous monks in Tibet to protest against Chinese rule.

> At Miss Smook's every character defined itself by the relation in which it stood to the power hierarchy. There were the bullies, there were the abject victims, and in between were those who played mixed roles of one sort and another … altogether my childhood taught me very effectively to understand the nature of totalitarianism. At the age of five I saw it in terms of the Sutton, but what I saw with the eyes of the spirit was the universal situation, the persecution of the minority, the crumbling away of decency and dignity, the day of the roughs.[9]

In this and similar passages of his autobiography, John Wain summed up the tragic view of life that was born of his helpless horror at outrages against minnows and 'acorn trees', and of the daily, wearing, strategy of dodging the mini-thugs of his nursery school. His is a most able account of a view that is held, consciously or otherwise, by large numbers of people, in which life is seen—shot through certainly with gleams of laughter and sense and tenderness—as essentially 'jungular' and

---

[9] John Wain, *Sprightly Running, Part of an Autobiography* (Macmillan, 1962), 24. Wain grew up on an estate, a 'colony of identical, raw-red, inharmonious houses, "the Sutton Dwellings" or, more simply "the Sutton".' *Sprightly Running*, 3.

predatory, a grim elbowing for survival on endless planes of existence.

If communities exist in virtue of a shared life and interest, then the nightmare half-truth of this picture can be ascribed to the lack of unified purpose which has reduced human society to a desert of individual and sectional interests in perpetual conflict and competition. Against this confusion the church sets its faith in the Christ event which has struck at the root of human bondage and opened the way to freedom by restoring true purpose to life. In Our Lord's brief reply to those who were trying to persuade him to go to Jerusalem, there is a deep glimpse into the mind of the Divine tactician whose actions are wholly deliberate and cannot be modified by any pressure. 'My time has not yet come, but your time is always here.' (John 7:6). In the divine timing of our salvation, the day of the toughs was met head on by the day of the Lord, and never again in its dwindling field of action in time and space can it escape the impact of that collision, which makes of every human choice a moment of crisis, whether to accept the life he came to give, or to be sucked deeper into the continuum of destructive self-interest.

In the first part of this essay an attempt was made to describe the place of intercessory prayer in a world on

its way back to wholeness through the acceptance of
Christ's mercy. We need now to have a closer look at
how this prayer is to be carried on as part of daily life.
John Wain, who was honest enough to follow out his
own perception to the narrowest and most searching
sphere he knew, found there, inside himself

> along with the easily-stifled impulse to help and the
> general paste of feelings, little hard lumps of evil, for
> there is a part of one's nature that identifies with the
> hunters against the hunted.[10]

It may need no very great courage or depth of self
knowledge to grasp the logic by which every greedy and
arrogant passion can be tracked home to its root in the
human heart; to see, for instance, that the insult to the
Divine Image in us, religiously sanctioned and thankfully
condoned in the apartheid policy of a great republic, is
reproduced in all the small slights offered by fear and
contempt to the immigrant neighbours in an English
street. It does however take courage to face this knowledge in its most intimate and personal applications; not
to grab at the comfort and reassurance of a burst of activity or protest, but to keep still and hold the knowledge
in the faith that these same greedy and arrogant passions
have been and are being met and judged by the Cross.

---

[10] Wain, *Sprightly Running*, 22.

To take one's stand in prayer at that point of weakness and exposure is to commit oneself to the conflict in which the Son of God overcame by love. It means going into the confusion and mess of life at the deepest level, or at least at that level of knowledge both of self and of evil will and intelligence that one is able to bear.

The Broken Heart

It is because contemplative prayer has nothing to do with the itch for experience, and everything to do with a patient and persevering will to receive truth and to be made love, that it is hard, dark, combative and boring. It confers not a sense of well-being or release, but a broken heart. Its sincerity is tested not in finding life a bit more bearable but in the willingness to keep coming back for more—for a deeper self knowledge and a further bearing of reality. The contradictions, false starts and setbacks by which a life of prayer develops, correspond quite simply to the basic paradoxes of the Christian faith—joy through suffering, life through death, victory through failure, peace through conflict— and the stifling negatives by which we know our remoteness from God have to be acknowledged and endured in dependence on God if they are to be healed and transfigured by the drawing of Divine Love.

The work of prayer undertaken seriously in the context of a busy life obviously demands times, however short, and places, however makeshift, of silence and withdrawal. It also needs tools, and the chief tool of prayer is the Bible. The common complaint that the language of religion is an irritating noise is only one way of saying what is true of many fields of discussion, that they suffer from that verbal inflation which has devalued speech and writing to the point where they can buy hardly a minute's attention. But the Bible itself, if not the panels and paperbacks which try to make it relevant is, above all, the place where words still mean something. It is a word-refuge, a word-hoard—in a sense a word-sanctuary. Words wait here in their strength, beyond the reach of fashion, ready to be met as if for the first time. Plain words—turn, offer, shepherd, face, water, light, name, city; quaint words—faithful, everlasting, Virgin, holy, worship, servant; discredited words—father, sin, obedience, fear; empty words—love, praise, spirit, new, heart—become in this setting imponderable, laden with meaning, able to be looked at.

It is above all in the Psalms that these words, already gateways into contemplation, become the spearheads of intercession as they gather and arrange themselves to speak for the needs of every human situation, to utter the human cry at the heart of every social and political problem. Words which are the food of the mind become also the support of the will when we as intercessors gather ourselves in dependence on the spirit who prays in us and in all the church, to plead for the darkness and disintegration of which we know we are part.

This feeding and focusing of faith and hope, this steady renewal of choice, is the heartbeat of prayer, and as it is strengthened and still the we begin to be aware that we have a small part to play in some operation, mysterious and yet assured, the scope of which we can only dimly grasp. We come to realize that our job is to stand where we are, in the darkness of faith, maintaining the heartbeat of prayer against whatever trivialities break our attention, whatever loveless pressures try to compel our involvement, and against the guerilla passions that would terrorize and inflame the matter of our prayer. By deliberately resting on the fact of God's love and reality we are enabled, through much failure, to recognize and to name these enemies, and by naming them to disarm them of the power to twist or enervate our intention.

To speak in these terms is to assume a state of war, with all its calls for a vigilance, gathered energy, and general fitness. So it is worth considering carefully the fighting outfit which Saint Paul recommends to the church at Ephesus:

Finally, be strong in the Lord and in the strength of his power. Put on the whole armour of God, so that you may be able to stand against the wiles of the devil. For our struggle is not against enemies of blood and flesh, but against the rulers, against the authorities, against the cosmic powers of this present darkness, against the spiritual forces of evil in the heavenly places. Therefore take up the whole armour of God, so that you may be able to withstand on that evil day, and having done everything, to stand firm. Stand therefore, and fasten the belt of truth around your waist, and put on the breastplate of righteousness. As shoes for your feet put on whatever will make you ready to proclaim the gospel of peace. With all of these, take the shield of faith, with which you will be able to quench all the flaming arrows of the evil one. Take the helmet of salvation, and the sword of the Spirit, which is the word of God. Pray in the Spirit at all times in every prayer and supplication. To that end keep alert and always persevere in supplication for all the saints.   (Eph. 6:10–18)

Clearly then, as Christians we have to be fully equipped in our prayer, as in our other work, to deal with reality, to cope with situations as they really are. To whatever category of being or non-being we may assign evil will and intelligence—and this is not the place to attempt it—eyes and ears and mind cannot ignore the terrible negativeness of their effects on every aspect of life—unless, indeed, by taking afternoons off in the Lotus-Land of an induced sense of beauty and reassurance.

The Kingdom

When the angel of the apocalypse cries out that 'The kingdom of the world has become the kingdom of our Lord and of his Messiah' (Rev. 11:15), he is referring to what will have been completed by Christ's members who, in time and space, will have made up in their own lives the sum total of his sufferings, who will have finished the work of reconciliation he gave them to do. It is this that gives such urgency to the here-and-now of Christian living.

In a description of the symbolism of the crown he designed for the investiture of the then Prince of Wales, the goldsmith Louis Osman said that the humble, intertwining motif of a crown of thorns constantly recurred to him as he worked and is faintly there in the finished crown.[11] The crown of thorns is the final paradox in the peace-making conflict of the Cross. It was

---

[11] Louis Osman, 'A Crown for Today', *The Times*, 1 July 1969.

rammed down on the head of the Servant King to clinch his humiliation and failure in the eyes of his fellow humans. It is both the agony and the great reward of those whose lives of service are offered in union with his offering—it should be noted that it can be worn inside as well as outside the establishment—and the intercessor dare not shift it in the battle of the mind.

The kingdoms of this world in which we have to function include not only the power complexes that in turn dominate and decay in history, but whatever can be defined by a common need or a common purpose as a society: rich or starving, criminal or law-abiding, peaceful or at war, permissive or totalitarian, alternative or straight. Not only these and all the rest, but also the chips and splinters of society, wedged with their meths bottles in derelict sites, crammed into refugee camps, tidied away in institutions, hanging about, drifting, hiding, dying. Given this vast responsibility of love for all, Christians are not concerned to identify themselves with any particular group at the expense of the others. The intention 'to put love in where love is not'[12] releases us from the struggle to communicate across barriers of age and ethic. The kingdom of our own

---

[12] St John of the Cross, letter to Sr María de la Encarnación, 6 July 1591.

particularity, our personal lives, our jobs, whatever they may be, provide us with all the raw material we need for being nailed to this intention and identified with all humankind at the point of need and weakness.

It is, after all, the same nest-building instinct that drives the squatters into empty flats and keeps the successful and well-to-do feverishly improving their houses. But is either place really home?

> Home is so sad, …
> A joyous shot at how things ought to be,
> Long fallen wide.[13]

Philip Larkin's words are true, in some sense, of every home, for the hunger and the disappointment and the emptiness at the bottom of things is the longing for God, for permanence, and it is in this radical human homelessness that we who are the guardians, the props, the dropouts and the victims of society, draw level.

Growth into Humanity

A group of students visiting one of the few churches that still functioned in Moscow in the Communist era, arrived one evening during the celebration of the liturgy.

---

[13] Philip Larkin, 'Home is so Sad' (1958).

While the priest was reassuring the congregation that these were Christians and friends, not a police raid, the visitors were looking around them at the church, brilliantly candlelit, and splendid with the strictly-ordered iconography of Orthodox tradition. Painted on the dome was the majestic figure of Christ, the Word of the Father and Lord of creation, overshadowed by the Holy Spirit, acknowledging with the gesture of his pierced hands the whole family of the redeemed as his own. Nearest to him were his human mother and the angelic and prophetic messengers of his incarnation; then the apostles and evangelists who took the good news to the poor of the Earth, and down the length of the walls witnesses to his love and reality in many societies: martyrs, doctors, pastors, men and women of heroic prayer. All these radiant figures encircle the congregation on the floor, an insignificant cluster of drab bulges with cheap clothes and tight scarves and worn faces.

Yet, between them and the grave rapture of the angels and saints there was the closest correspondence, an intimate unity of purpose and understanding, for these were the heavenly citizens coming down in their hosts to encourage and support the pilgrim church that is moving towards full humanity in Christ through the desert of modern life. Here the outlines of meaning were sharpened by the absence of affluence and security, for this, and not the continuum of trampling and being trampled, is the universal situation. The lives of these people were hard and restricted, and as overt Christians in a Communist state their prospects of social and material betterment were of the dimmest, but those who, that night, were witnesses of their joy in the fellowship of the eucharistic meal knew that they were not looking at the solidarity of an oppressed minority driven together by a shared desperation but at the life of the kingdom, which in time and space is expressed in the patience and staying power of the people of God.

Such glimpses of the church, charged with presence and purpose and destiny, is a rebuke to our lack of joy and peace in believing, and to the spiritual diffidence which, in the anxiety to allow for every point of view, cannot bring itself to say outright, *Christ is the light of the world, and all your needs and desires are met in him.*[14] But to say this means asking for a costly response. As long as animal love and togetherness, animal freedom to be oneself, is the ceiling of desire, the struggle to secure them for everyone will be more than enough to absorb all our energies forever; and where the struggle is on the lowest terms of all, even animal survival will

---

[14] Cf. Phil. 4:19.

be 'almost happiness' as it was for Ivan Denisovitch at the end of the day.[15] But God made us for something we have hardly begun to want: everlasting blessedness in union with him. Between the pursuit of happiness and the gift of joy there takes place a radical change of direction. By asking a woman for a drink, Jesus was able to awaken her to the undreamed-of possibility of that joy, and from the knowledge of her emptiness to draw out the response, 'Sir, give me this water.' (John 4:15).

Those bluntly-labelled instruments of mercy such as 'shelter', 'release', and many more, express a direct contemporary response to the timeless imperatives of the gospel, which are the only touchstone of love that acts. Prayer that grows in grief for sin and separation as it fixes its gaze steadily on the real, the lasting and the holy, is tested by the lengths to which it will go in self-giving for others. But equally those who persevere in prayer, even when it seems useless, and by that very doggedness are carrying the battle into the field of spiritual combat and learning to stand there, have a quality and fibre to bring to their love-in-action which it might otherwise lack. The compassion that is deepened and ordered in

---

[15] Alexsandr Solzhenitsyn, *One Day in the Life of Ivan Denisovich*, trans. Ralph Parker, Penguin Modern Classics (Penguin, 2000).

prayer cannot stop short at comforting and alleviating but must go on to offer the creative friendship which cares so deeply for the fulfilment of another that it will do nothing to shield them from that painful growth through loneliness, privation and fear, into the humanity which Christ has won for us and for which we are increasingly enabled. 'I am the food of full-grown men. Grow up and you shall feed on me' was Christ's word to St Augustine.[16] Fullness, wholeness and newness of life as it is offered to each one of us by, with, and in Christ, is the end in view of all intercessory prayer.

> Lord hold my will, enlighten me
> That I may hold my self so still
> To be true penitence and so receive
> The mercy offered me –
> To be made one with love
> To pray love's prayer for unity.[17]

---

[16] St Augustine, *Confessions*, trans. Edward B. Pusey (Collier Books, 1961), VII.10.

[17] Gilbert Shaw, *Sitio 'I Thirst': Prayers of Intercession* (SLG Press, 1970), 47.

SLG PRESS PUBLICATIONS

SLG Pocket Books

The Reconcilers, Sister Isabel SLG
From Witness to Compassion, Kevin Parkes

Fairacres Publications

Prayer and the Life of Reconciliation, Gilbert Shaw
Aloneness not Loneliness, Mother Mary Clare SLG
Intercession, Mother Mary Clare SLG
Prayer: Extracts from the Teaching of Father Gilbert Shaw, Gilbert Shaw
Learning to Pray, Mother Mary Clare SLG
Death, the Gateway to Life, Gilbert Shaw
The Victory of the Cross, Dumitru Stăniloae
The Message of Saint Seraphim, Irina Gorainov
Julian of Norwich: Four Studies to Commemorate the Sixth Centenary of the Revelations of Divine Love, Sister Benedicta Ward SLG, Sister Eileen Mary SLG, Sister Mary Paul SLG, A. M. Allchin
The Power of the Name: The Jesus Prayer in Orthodox Spirituality, Kallistos Ware
Prayer and Contemplation and Distractions are for Healing, Robert Llewelyn
The Wisdom of the Desert Fathers, trans. Sister Benedicta Ward SLG
Letters of Saint Antony the Great, trans. Derwas Chitty
From Loneliness to Solitude, Roland Walls
Theology and Spirituality, Andrew Louth
Kabir: The Way of Love and Paradox, Sister Rosemary SLG
Anselm of Canterbury: A Monastic Scholar, Sister Benedicta Ward SLG
Mary and the Mystery of the Incarnation: An Essay on the Mother of God in the Theology of Karl Barth, Andrew Louth
Trinity and Incarnation in Anglican Tradition, A. M. Allchin
Facing Depression, Gonville ffrench-Beytagh
The Single Person, Philip Welsh
The Letters of Ammonas, Successor of St Antony, trans. Derwas Chitty, introd. Sebastian Brock
George Herbert, Priest and Poet, Kenneth Mason
A Study of Wisdom: Three Tracts by the Author of The Cloud of Unknowing, trans. Clifton Wolters

The Psalms: Prayer Book of the Bible, Dietrich Bonhoeffer, trans. Sister Isabel SLG

Prayer & Holiness: The Icon of Man Renewed in God, Dumitru Stăniloae

Walter Hilton: Eight Chapters on Perfection & Angels' Song, trans. Rosemary Dorward

Creative Suffering, Iulia de Beausobre

Bringing Forth Christ: Five Feasts of the Child Jesus by St Bonaventure, trans. Eric Doyle OFM

Gentleness in John of the Cross, Thomas Kane

Saint Gregory Nazianzen: Selected Poems, trans. John McGuckin

The World of the Desert Fathers: Stories and Sayings from the Anonymous Series of the Apophthegmata Patrum, trans. Columba Stewart OSB

Growing Old with God, Timothy N. Rudd

Julian Reconsidered, Kenneth Leech, Sister Benedicta Ward SLG

The Unicorn: Meditations on the Love of God, Harry Galbraith Miller

The Creativity of Diminishment, Sister Anke

Called to be Priests, Hugh Wybrew

A Kind of Watershed: An Anglican Lay View of Sacramental Confession, Christine North

Jesus, the Living Lord, Bishop Michael Ramsey

The Monastic Letters of Saint Athanasius the Great, trans. and introd. Leslie Barnard

The Hidden Joy, Sister Jane SLG, ed. Dorothy Sutherland (

Prayer of the Heart: An Approach to Silent Prayer and Prayer in the Night, Alexander Ryrie

Evelyn Underhill, Anglican Mystic: Two Centenary Essays, A. M. Allchin, Bishop Michael Ramsey

Apostolate and the Mirrors of Paradox, Sydney Evans, ed. Andrew Linzey & Brian Horne

The Wisdom of Saint Isaac the Syrian, Sebastian Brock

Saint Thérèse of Lisieux: Her Relevance for Today, Sister Eileen Mary SLG

Expectations: Five Addresses for Those Beginning Ministry, Sister Edmée SLG

Scenes from Animal Life: Fables for the Enneagram Types, Waltraud Kirschke, trans. Sister Isabel SLG

Praying the Word of God: The Use of Lectio Divina, Charles Dumont OCSO

Love Unknown: Meditations on the Death and Resurrection of Jesus, John Barton

The Hidden Way of Love: Jean-Pierre de Caussade's Spirituality of Abandonment, Barry Conaway

Shepherd and Servant: The Spiritual Theology of Saint Dunstan, Douglas Dales

Pilgrimage of the Heart, Sister Benedicta Ward SLG

Contemplative Church: Pondering Church in Challenging Times, Andy Lord
Stations of the Cross, Donald McChesney, Jean-Bernard Lalanne
Being Christian among Britain's Muslims, Nicholas Heale
Create in me a Clean Heart, James Coutts
Instruments of the Passion, Lucy McKitterick
People with Dementia as Teachers of Faith, Regina Schlingheider
Faces in the Crowd, Tony Dickinson

www.slgpress.co.uk